Farming, Faith, & Family Life

STEPHEN WOOD

Family Life Center Publications

Copyright © 2016 Family Life Center Publications

All rights reserved. No part of this book may be reproduced or transmitted in any form or by any means, electronic or mechanical, including photocopying, recording or by any information storage or retrieval system, without permission in writing from the publisher.

ISBN: 978-0-9821666-1-1

Library of Congress Control Number: 2016950985
Book production: Family Life Center Publications
Cover and layout design: 5sparrows.com
Manufactured in the United States of America

Unless otherwise indicated, Scripture quotations are taken from the Revised Standard Version, Catholic Edition [RSVCE], copyright © 1965 and 1966 by the Division of Christian Education of the National Council of the Churches of Christ in the United States of America. Used by permission.

Family Life Center Publications
2130 Wade Hampton Blvd.
Greenville, SC 29615
www.Dads.org

Contents

Foreword................................9

PART I
*Why a Christian Family
Should Consider Farming* 13

PART II
How a Family Can Begin Farming.............27

Endnotes................................57

Recommended Reading 61

Dedication

To my father, John Kirk Wood,
who taught me the love of farming,

and

To Allan Carlson,
for helping to awaken that love

Praise for *Farming, Faith, and Family Life*

In this splendid booklet, Stephen Wood explains both the 'Why' and 'How' of the Christian Home on the Farm. In making this argument, he joins a strong line of Catholic teachers. 'The farm is the natural habitat of the family,' wrote Fr. Edwin V. O'Hara, the founder of the National Catholic Rural Life Conference, in 1920; 'on the farm alone, …the economic forces work for the unity of the family.' Wood amplifies this idea, showing that the "refunctionalizing" of home life is a necessary step toward both family renewal and the restoration of a Christian culture in this land. He also includes delightful commentaries on "farmschooling" (a homeschool in the country) and "grandfarming" (a place where grandparents can contribute meaningfully to the spiritual and physical formation of their grandchildren). Wood concludes with sound practical advice on how and where to launch a new family farm. In short, this booklet is a rich gift to all Christian parents…. and grandparents!

–ALLAN C. CARLSON, Founder and President Emeritus, The Howard Center for Family, Religion & Society and author of *The Natural Family Where It Belongs: New Agrarian Essays*

Foreword

Several years ago, Steve Wood and I discovered that we had a common interest in small farming, but I had no idea to what extent he had come about this interest naturally, through the God-given gift of a childhood on a farm and within a farm family. All of my interest and learning about farming, husbandry, and even gardening came about in later life, mostly through books and concurrent with diminishing brain cells! For these and more reasons, I highly enjoyed and recommend Steve's short primer, *Farming, Faith, and Family Life*.

There are literally hundreds if not thousands of books, magazines, blogs, and websites dedicated to all aspects of farming and back-to-the-land rural living. To spend one's time trying to read, decipher, summarize, and strategize from even a fraction of these sources would surely eliminate any time for actually getting outside and starting. Trust me; I tried it! For your interest and benefit, Steve has done you a great favor: he has provided a well-tested primer of the "who, what, where, when, why, and hows" of sticking one's toe into the water of small farming. He begins with theory as well as theology, and particularly, with the complementary commingling of homeschooling and rural life. He then ends with a nice introductory summary, from all the authors he's read and visited, of a few key steps to take if one feels at least a little moved to venture forward.

Where he concludes his booklet, however, hit closest to home, when he discusses "Grandfarming," for this is exactly why my wife and I are presently contemplating focusing even more of our time and effort in our graying years on our small farm. It isn't about retirement or about seeking avenues for more income; it's about what we can best provide for our children and grandchildren in the next five, ten, twenty years of their lives, and ours. What better place to nurture them than on a farm with critters to pet or ride, a pond to fish and swim, and great food to pick and eat!

Of course, farming and farm life is a vocation like any other. Is it possible God is calling you to consider a simpler life away from the fast-paced, technology-driven, progress-crazed, nature-deprived culture of modern urban living? As Steve suggests, it can begin with a small box of soil and vegetables under a window, or maybe a drive into the country, or maybe visiting a few websites about rural living, or maybe attending a seminar. But in the end, it involves praying together with your spouse: Where do you want your family to be in five, ten, twenty years? Where do you think our country, our world, is going to be in five, ten, twenty years, and where do you think the best place for your family will be, come what may?

Steve's book will only take an hour or so to read, but it may be an hour God can use to change the direction of your family's life.

—MARCUS GRODI, author of *Life from Our Land: The Search for a Simpler Life in a Complex World*

Part 1

WHY A CHRISTIAN FAMILY SHOULD CONSIDER FARMING

What if I had it all to do over again? What significant change would I make in my fathering and family life?

I hesitate to recommend something I've never practiced, but what I'm recommending I have experienced. It was a place called Woodlane Farm, in Allentown, Pennsylvania. My dad, a businessman, spent his childhood summers working on farms in Iowa. My mother loved horses. The two of them came up with the idea that a farm would be a great place to raise a family. It was.

Our farm consisted of seventy acres of land, fifty head of Angus cattle, about a dozen horses and ponies, lots of cats and dogs, and at times chickens, pigs, and rabbits. We grew corn and hay on the seventy acres, in addition to nearby fields that we leased. In hay season, the workday started at seven. We ate in the fields and worked until dark. My dad was a friend of the local high school football coach, and he hired the entire team during hay season. Slinging fifty-pound bales of hay for ten hours a day was a legal way to get the team conditioned before the official season began.

I started driving tractors when I was about eight years old. During the winters, I'd get up before dawn to thaw water faucets and feed the animals. After football and basketball practices I worked past dark, feeding the animals. When I was twelve years old, I had sole responsibility during the week for feeding over sixty animals and maintaining the farm. I had a 1949 Willis Jeep (the kind John Wayne drove in WWII movies!) to fulfill my responsibilities.

At the time, my brother and I complained continually that we were victims of slave labor, but I can't imagine a richer, fuller, more educational and more character-building experience than growing up on a farm.

When my dad hung up his business suit and put on his old Navy shirt, blue jeans, and boots, our dogs and we kids got excited. It was time for farm work.

Why a Christian Family Should Consider Farming

One Saturday my mother, fearing that I was missing out on "normal" city activities, told me that she had arranged for me to attend a birthday party in town. I broke into tears. Puzzled by my reaction, she asked what was wrong. I said, "I want to work with Dad!" Pin-the-tail-on-the-donkey and birthday cakes couldn't hold a candle to sweat, challenge, mud, dogs, tractors, and working with Dad on a farm.

I consider my ten years on the farm the most formative years in my preparation for Christian service. Yes, I place a high value on my theological education, but seminary doesn't begin to prepare you for launching a worldwide apostolate with $507. Farm life does. On the farm you have a job to do, and you have to figure out how to accomplish it with the strength you have and the tools at your disposal. A farm is the best training ground for any calling in life.

I made one stab at getting back to a farm before I was married, but distance and the time demands of youth ministry made dual careers impossible. I sold my acreage to finance my seminary education.

Farming, Faith, & Family Life

A turning point in both my youth ministry and my subsequent family ministry was at a youth drug-prevention seminar at Columbia Medical School during the 1970s. Presented to the seminar were the results of the most comprehensive youth survey in the history of the world. I learned two things from the presidential appointee presenting the results, yet I acted on only one of them.

First, I learned that the most effective way to prevent drug abuse was to replace peer pressure with parental pressure. Increasing parental involvement in the lives of children and youth was found to be the very best method of preventing drug addiction. This knowledge profoundly affected me. It was the start of my decades-long emphasis on parents as the ideal youth workers.

Second, towards the end of his talk, he mentioned something I wish I had acted on. This Washington Beltway bigwig had resigned his presidential appointment and purchased a farm. He realized that a farm was the ideal setting for replacing peer pressure with parental pressure. Work life and family life, segregated in cities, are integrated on a farm. Parents and children, so torn apart in suburbia, are melded together on a farm.

Why a Christian Family Should Consider Farming

To me, having a dual career as both a minister and a farmer seemed impossible. Maybe it was, and then again, maybe it wasn't. It's amazing what anyone can accomplish if the perceived value and importance is high enough. Your priority for a rural family life will depend, in part, upon your analysis of our times and culture.

A family interested in farming will profit by reading what Catholic leaders have said about rural life.[1] Here is what Pope Pius XII said to farmers about farm life:

> More than anyone else you live in continual contact with nature. It is actual contact, since your lives are lived in places still remote from the excesses of an artificial civilization. Under the sun of the Heavenly Father your lives are dedicated to bringing forth from the depths of the earth the abundant riches which His hand has hidden there for you. Your families are not merely consumer-communities, but also, and especially, producer-communities.
>
> Your lives are rooted in the family—universally, deeply, and completely; consequently, they conform very closely to nature. In this fact lie your economic strength and your ability

to withstand adversity in critical times. Your being so strongly rooted in the family constitutes the importance of your contribution to the correct development of the private and public order of society. You are called upon for this reason to perform an indispensable function as source and defense of a stainless moral and religious life. For the land is a kind of nursery which supplies men, sound in soul and body, for all occupations, for the Church, and for the State.

With all our heart, dear sons, we invoke heaven's choicest blessings on you and on your families. The Church has always blessed you in a particular manner, and in many ways has brought your working year into her liturgical year. We invoke these blessings upon the work of your hands, from which the holy altar of God receives the bread and wine. May the Lord give you, in the words of Holy Scripture, "the dew of heaven, and of the fatness of the earth, abundance of corn and wine!" (Gen. 27:28)[2]

So how could this work in our modern world? For many, the farm option is not even a remote possibility. For you there's no need to worry, remembering that godly families, not farms, are what's critical for the raising of godly children. For others, a farm might indeed be a possibility, even if you initially think it impractical and impossible.

It isn't necessary to make the farm your primary source of income, especially if you don't yet own land, or have experience with farming. I'm not a "return to the land" purist. Instead, I'm a realist, since less than 10 percent of farm families can rely solely on their farm income.[3] A recent assessment described the economic condition of many families in the New Catholic Land Movement as "grim." So be cautious about prematurely quitting your job and heading to rural country.

Ideally, you could combine a high-tech, or other highly skilled, career with your small working farm. Four diverse career examples of fathers with small farms include: a job reading and analyzing spy satellite photos; a Christian life coach who uses a cell phone from an old hunting cabin on his farm; an EWTN TV host who tends cows before taping television and radio episodes; and an architect/builder who manages construction jobs with a smartphone in his pastures.

Be careful about the specialty you select. The same opportunity that allows you to work at home on the farm may allow profit-seeking corporations in a global economy to take work overseas. Many middle-class job opportunities are disappearing at an alarming rate. Don't choose something that can be easily exported overseas.

There's no need to make your farm a complicated venture requiring huge silos, vast acreage, expensive equipment, and labor-consuming operations. Simplicity works fine. I would also avoid utopian rural-life co-ops, for the simple reason that so many never work.[4] Sure, encourage other Christian families to move into your rural region, but keep ownership and legal structure simple, separate, and unencumbered.

Today, as I am raising sheep while working in another job, I want something small and easy to operate. I don't see the need for a farm enterprise to be nearly as extensive as the one my father had. Even though my dad had fifty head of cattle, I'd be content with a smaller number of livestock. Part II of this booklet will suggest some sustainable ways to make farming your primary income, if that is your desire.

Your family-formation goal in farming is to have family farm work that results in the real production of a few things needed by the household. This results in "refunctionalizing" the family in the area of work.

Refunctionalizing the family

What is "refunctionalizing"? Briefly, refunctionalizing a family means restoring the natural activities of family life lost through: industrialization; governmental take-over of family responsibilities, including education; corporate life snuffing out family businesses and family farms; and modern consumerism.

When a family refunctionalizes in any single area, it has a transforming effect on other facets of family life. Therefore, something as simple as combining homeschooling with work on a family farm has a unique potential to benefit family life.

Debt-free farm life

Another benefit of a smaller operation is that you don't need to load up on debt for your farm. Living on too much credit is a mistake. Debt has put countless family farms out of business during the past fifty years.

A wholesome place to raise children

Where you choose to live is important for the formation of your children. St. Thomas More considered his thirty-two acre farm in the English countryside to be a more wholesome environment for raising his family than London's fine neighborhoods and elite social circles. Pope Pius XII warned that in the city a man loses "his happiness, his honor, and his very soul."[5] Geographically, seek a balance, where you are far enough away to farm, yet close enough to participate in a parish and have stores nearby for necessary shopping.[6]

The mistakes of earlier agrarian movements

The saying, "Those who fail to learn history are doomed to repeat it" is assuredly true when it comes to agrarian experiments. In order to keep your family from becoming a "return to the land" casualty, I recommend reading Allan Carlson's books on the effects of the industrial revolution on the family, his analysis of the strengths and weaknesses of twentieth-century agrarian movements, and his insights on the ability of homeschooling to "refunctionalize" the family in ways the agrarian movement failed to do.[7] For instance, the agrarians knew that family fertility was a sign of a "refunctionalized" family. In Canada, the fertility of homeschoolers is twice the national average.[8]

Therefore, the size and type of farming you do may not be nearly as important as embracing religiously motivated homeschooling.[9] As Carlson summarizes: "It would be the radical, albeit simple act of parents teaching their own children in their own dwellings that would turn out to be the key to recreating working homes."[10]

Farming, Faith, & Family Life

Farmschooling

I believe that the very best potential for reuniting contemporary Christian families with farm life is the homeschooling movement. With minimal ecclesiastical and civil support, the homeschooling movement has successfully reunited home life with education. This major achievement is often accomplished in families supported by a single paycheck. The fruits of homeschooling are closer family bonds, higher academic achievement, lower dependence upon the peer group, and an increase in faith knowledge and practice. And remember—all this was accomplished without tax-funded state support.

Homeschooling families have the smallest step to take to become a farm family over any other demographic group that I can think of. They have already achieved "refunctionalizing" their families in ways that the twentieth-century agrarian movements failed to accomplish due to their excessive dependence upon government aid. Building on the success of the homeschooling movement is a wise path to a future where family and faith find deep roots in farm life.

Preserving and restoring Christian culture

More is needed for a contemporary return to Catholic rural life than just a nostalgic desire "to get back to the land." The impulse for a new agrarian movement needs to be a religiously motivated desire to save our families and to restore Christian culture. Along with the teaching of Pope Pius XII on rural life cited earlier, the challenging insight of John Senior is critical to restoring Christian culture:

> If we are to restore an authentic Christian Humanism, in the wide sense of Christian Culture, we shall have to think not just about fighting infanticide, sex education and pornography, which are the front lines of Secular Humanism—by all means fight them to the death—but the positive work of the restoration of culture which lies wrecked in the wake of the humanist assault. We shall have to think about simpler, larger, elemental things which are the foundation and principle of the superstructures we must rebuild. We shall have to think about work, the kind of work by

which we earn our daily bread, and especially farming as the only true basis of economic and social life. God made the country, man made the town . . .

We become the work we do. If farming reflects Divine attributes, farmers through their work become something like God. Appearances are not only signs of reality but in a sense are like sacraments; they effect what they signify. I mean that there is a cause-effect relation between the work we do, the clothes we wear or do not wear, the houses we live in, the walls or lack of walls, the landscape, the semi-conscious sights, sounds, smells, tastes and touches of our ordinary lives—a close connection between these and the moral and spiritual development of souls.[11]

The finest place on earth for a family

Monsignor Luigi Ligutti (1895–1983), the tireless advocate for Catholic rural life, expressed the highest motivation for a family to adopt farm life:

> [The farm is] the finest place on earth for a family to prepare for heaven.[12]

Part Two
How a Family Can Begin Farming

New car or new farm?

You might ask, "How can an average middle-class family begin farming?" You might be surprised to learn that a family can begin the adventure of becoming a farm family for about the price of a new car. Sound interesting?

When thinking of buying and launching a farm operation, most people imagine cash or debt requirements upwards of a quarter million dollars. There are exorbitant land costs, tractors, bailers, plows, tillers, planters, silos, repeated applications of chemical fertilizers, costs of livestock, constant applications of antibiotics, and more. For most families, these investments are unthinkably expensive and far beyond their reach.

What if I told you that there is an entirely different way to farm that doesn't require indebtedness for all the investments and agricultural inputs mentioned above? The good news is, that in the midst of farm bankruptcies and the staggering losses of family farms, there is an economical way that your family can establish a farmstead.

Intelligent Design Farming

One of the most exciting scientific and intellectual developments over the past quarter-century has been the Intelligent Design movement. In *Darwin's Black Box,* Professor Michael Behe of Lehigh University shows how use of the electron microscope has revealed the incredibly integrated complexity in what has been mislabeled the "simple" cell.

Likewise, Stephen Meyers, a Ph.D. from the University of Cambridge in the philosophy of science, describes in his book, *Signature in the Cell: DNA and the Evidence for Intelligent Design,* the amazing complexity discovered in the design of DNA. At first Meyers noticed a similarity between advanced computer code and DNA. Upon further investigation he concluded that DNA is significantly more complex than the most sophisticated computer code. Meyers, in both *Signature in the Cell*, and his new book, *Darwin on Trial*, provides convincing evidence that the complexity of DNA as an information code couldn't have just happened—rather, it was intelligently designed.

Beliefs have widespread consequences in both culture and cultivation. C.S. Lewis warned, "The Dying God has no place in chemical agriculture."[13] To reverse unnatural corporate/chemical agriculture we need more than worthwhile educational efforts and a change in shopping habits. We need a recovery of the foundational belief in God's direct and intelligent creation of our world.

Modern practices such as industrial farming with GMOs (genetically modified organisms); overuse of chemical fertilizers; disease-filled crowded feedlots; abuse of herbicides, insecticides, and antibiotics; grains instead of grasses fed to herbivores; monocultures; debt-financed mega-machinery; and mineral-deficient food are all essentially impositions of unintelligent human design upon the land, plants, and animals. I came away from watching the DVD, *Food, Inc.*, with the thought that J.R.R. Tolkien's Orcs must have escaped from Mordor to create our modern system of global corporate agriculture.

Rather than imposing industrial systems upon agriculture, Intelligent Design Farming seeks to discover and wisely follow the divine blueprint revealed in nature that is staring us in the face.

Intelligent Design Farming:

- Observes and imitates the systems displayed in nature

- Consciously seeks to work in harmony with nature, rather than fight against it

- Uses your head just as much as your back when farming

- Avoids unnecessary farm expenses for equipment, chemical fertilizers, and antibiotics

- Encourages freedom by not becoming a debt-slave, or a servant of *Food, Inc.*

- Reaps profitability with thanksgiving for God's generous gift of photosynthesis, which brings increase from the land

Certainly many, if not most, of the growing number of contemporary farmers practicing

Intelligent Design Farming may not formally adhere to the Intelligent Design school of origins, but what they are doing in practice is extrapolating profitable agricultural systems from a careful observation of design in nature.

Right now you might be asking yourself, "Do these lofty principles of Intelligent Design Farming actually work?" A tour of three fascinating farms will answer this question.

The bankrupt farmer who now controls 12 farms

Greg Judy, of Green Pastures Farms in Missouri, is a fascinating Intelligent Design Farmer. In 1996, Mr. Judy was facing a rapidly approaching bankruptcy and was forced to liquidate his cow herd to pay farm debts. A year later he was completely broke. It was then that he encountered an enlightening quote that would dramatically transform both his farming practices and his finances.

Greg Judy read in *The Stockman Grass Farmer* magazine this quotation from its editor: "Your sole purpose should be not to own the land, but to make a living from the land." Judy realized that he could graze cattle on well-managed grass pastures that were leased instead of owned. Within three years Judy was able to pay off his entire home and farm loans. Today, he successfully manages twelve leased farms, and grazes more than 1,100 head of cattle, sheep, and goats on 1,560 acres.

What I find most amazing about Greg Judy's management of twelve debt-free farms is that his only farm equipment is a single ATV. That's it. His profitable multi-farm operation requires no tractors, combines, plows, silos, or bailers.

Greg Judy's hard-learned lessons have opened a path for any middle-class family to begin farming on near-by leased land. The average age of farmers in the United States is fifty-seven and climbing. As American farmers age and their children abandon farming for the city, they are often eager to find a young family to lease and work the land they have labored on for a lifetime. Investors who own large tracts of agricultural land for eventual development are also good candidates for a leased grazing operation. Hunters owning large acreage will find deer with

How a Family Can Begin Farming

larger antlers and other animals thriving on well-managed intensive-grazing acreage.

The main costs for grazing on leased land are the cost of fencing, water lines, guard animals, and the livestock themselves. Judy enthusiastically relates the benefits of St. Croix hair sheep: they don't need shearing, give birth easily, are fertile, parasite-resistant, and cost far less than cattle.

Judy enjoys sharing how his hair sheep consume and kill parasites particular to cattle. Likewise, his cattle consume and kill parasites harmful to sheep. This symbiotic relationship between sheep and cattle is just one example of the countless other beneficial relationships stemming from multi-species Intelligent Design Farming. Remember that God has created plants and animals in a grand harmonious relationship. The *Catechism of the Catholic Church* explains that it is up to us to discover these relationships:

> Creatures exist only in dependence on each other, to complete each other, in the service of each other. The order and harmony of the created world results from the diversity of beings and from the relationships which exist among them. Man discovers them progressively as the laws of nature. – Sections 340-41

Along with realizing that a farmer can find financial success by leasing rather than owning land, Greg Judy acted upon the realization that cattle are created as herbivores; that is, animals physiologically adapted to eating plants, especially grass, as the main source of their diet. The modern cattle industry relies upon grains instead of grasses. This costly mistake is a primary cause for the failure of family cattle operations. Grains and other feed can consume as much as two-thirds of a farm's income. Add in antibiotics, herbicides, and insecticides, and the small farmer is left with little-to-nothing.

Judy explains that financial success in raising cattle can be achieved by studying bison as they were before the American plains were plowed under. The buffalo grazed in tight protective groups (herds) and were continually on the move. The first pioneers to see the American plains were astonished to find grass growing as tall as the top of a man on a horse thanks to the beneficial grazing habits of bison, elk, antelope, and deer.

Judy and other successful grass farmers imitate the bison's habits by frequently moving cattle and sheep from one small paddock to another. This is called rotational mob-grazing. It is the natural feeding pattern for herbivores. His South Poll cattle, members of a heat-tolerant maternal breed that's efficient for converting rich pasture grass to tender beef, thrive as a result of his rotational mob-grazing management system.

When the cattle have the opportunity to eat only the highly nutritious and delicious top portion of pasture grasses, it stimulates overall plant growth. Have you ever pruned just a few branches off a rose bush and noticed those branches surge in growth much more than the uncut branches? Something similar happens when livestock are allowed to snip only the top portion of grasses and then are moved to a new paddock. The idea is to frequently move livestock between several smaller paddocks rather than just letting them graze on a few large pastures for long periods.

Jesus said, "Every branch that does bear fruit he prunes, that it may bear more fruit" (John 15:2). What the vinedresser does in pruning the vineyard to increase fruit-bearing, cattle and sheep do by clipping the top of the grass without the need for any human labor. In addition, livestock naturally bunched together while grazing will also crush some of the uneaten grass into the ground, adding carbon to the pasture. Urine and poop from cattle and sheep provide a natural soil-creating and soil-enriching fertilizer.

Besides reading both of Greg Judy's books, it might be wise to attend his Mob Grazing School at his Green Pastures Farm.[14] If you are a young person seriously interested in farming, Greg Judy offers a valuable internship where you can get on-the-job training from an amazingly intelligent farmer who has discovered the simplicity of successful farming.

The Happy Cow Dairyman

In 1989, Tom Trantham, a well-known and experienced South Carolina dairyman, faced foreclosure. Feed costs were eating up all his profits. Around the time for him to sign the foreclosure papers his dairy herd broke down a fence and escaped into one of his pastures. He was so discouraged by the prospect of losing his farm and so mad at his cattle for breaking out that he left them in the pasture all day.

How a Family Can Begin Farming

When it came time for the evening milking he wasn't expecting much, since his dairy cows didn't have what he thought was their necessary grain. To his shock, the cows produced much more milk than normal. Sensing something unusual about a grass diet, he allowed his cattle to enjoy another day of eating only grass. You can guess what happened: an abundance of milk. Cows fed nutrient-rich grass are happy cows—and happy cows provide generous quantities of milk.

A few years after Tom's discovery, researchers at nearby Clemson University got interested in what was going on at what is now called his 12 Aprils Dairy.[15] What the Clemson researchers and Tom Trantham developed was a method of dairy farming where cattle are fed grass, using a system of rotational mob-grazing through a series of twenty-nine paddocks. The result, aided by South Carolina's gentle weather and generous rainfall, was a year-round provision of lush green April-like pastures.

Folks from around the United States and even from foreign countries are visiting the 12 Aprils Dairy and the adjoining Happy Cow Creamery.

During the farm tour, you'll sense that Tom Trantham is a happy man today, just like his cows. Due to his financial success, two of his adult children have been able to join him in full-time work in the creamery and dairy.

While visiting the farm each guest is offered a sample of Happy Cow milk by Mrs. Trantham. The taste test of the chocolate milk is worth the effort of an out-of-state visit.

Besides using intelligent agricultural practices, Tom is a skilled entrepreneur. With a twinkle in his eye, he gives some sage business advice to any prospective grass farmer. "You can't make a profit when the corporations keep 90 percent of the profit and you keep 10 percent." Fortunately, local food movements are creating a market to make sustainable small-scale agriculture a real possibility.

Before we leave the 12 Aprils Dairy, I must tell you about the soil in their pastures. Tom took our tour group into his pastures to meet his happy cows. He reached down and picked up a handful of dirt and told us to look at what rotational mob-grazing does to the soil. I couldn't believe my eyes. It was like looking at the most expensive premium potting mix that you buy at a garden center. It looked so unbelievably rich, dark, moist, and uncompressed that I thought maybe I was being conned. I had never seen such soil in South Carolina. So I began looking around the pasture to ensure that what I was seeing was characteristic of the entire pasture. It was.

What made all of this so unusual to me was the memory of planting my first tree on my South Carolina property years earlier. When I tried pushing a shovel into the hard red clay it didn't budge, so I took a pick and slammed it down as hard as I could. When I started bending the pick backwards it bent 180 degrees and the soil barely moved. The soil on my property had been neglected and depleted for years before our arrival, just like many other South Carolina properties.

Although I had read books and articles and attended lectures on the soil-building and enriching effects of rotational mob-grazing, seeing what Tom Trantham has accomplished with his soil seemed miraculous. I don't recommend dairy farming to most families because of the unique needs of dairies, especially the year-round twice-a-day milking. Yet, every prospective farming family needs to see the 12 Aprils Dairy, either by the online visitor's video, or an in-person visit.

This story about Tom Trantham's happy cows helps explain why hundreds of families are seeking to purchase their milk from his grass-fed dairy. Once when 12 Aprils Dairy sent a sample of their milk off to the university to have it tested for nutrient content, they received an apologetic call from the lab saying their calibrations must be off since the test results were so unusual. So the dairy sent a second sample, and this time the university realized it wasn't the calibrations, but the nutrient content from the Happy Cow Creamery that was literally off the charts.

It's worth reading the grateful testimonials on the Happy Cow Creamery website describing the health benefits from drinking truly nutritious milk.[16] Following nature's design for herbivores makes for happy cows, happy pastures, happy dairymen, and smiling healthy people.

How a Family Can Begin Farming

The lunatic farmer building a family legacy

It's hard to categorize Joel Salatin who describes himself as a "Christian-libertarian-environmentalist-capitalist-lunatic-farmer." Future farming families everywhere should be thankful that the mold was thrown away when Joel Salatin was created. He is the quintessential independent thinker, innovator, and local food entrepreneur. Joel is the personification of the Jeffersonian intellectual agrarian.

Many folks became acquainted with Joel Salatin and his Polyface Farms in the documentary films *Food, Inc.* and *Fresh*. He was also featured in the widely read *The Omnivore's Dilemma* by Michael Pollen.

Salatin is the author of eight books filled with wit, wisdom, and countless natural farming how-to's for any current or prospective farming family. He lives and works on a 550-acre family-owned farm in the Shenandoah Valley of Virginia. The farm offers tours, apprenticeships, an informative website, instructional DVDs, and online streaming of farming classes. Polyface Farms is perhaps the best one-stop place in America to learn how to pasture-raise healthy cattle, chickens, turkeys, and pigs.[17]

Growing natural food is only one step in a two-step process of affordable farming. Family farmers need to be entrepreneurs if they want to avoid going broke as the corporate food industry gobbles up their profits. Salatin has developed successful ways to sell all his products directly to local consumers and restaurants.

Salatin is the epitome of an Intelligent Design Farmer. His website states that he believes that "the Creator's design is still the best pattern for the biological world." A typical Salatin witticism reflecting his philosophy of farming exhorts us to respect and honor through farm practices "the pigness of the pig."

The *Catechism of the Catholic Church*, in a more elaborate, but similar fashion, says:

> Each creature possesses its own particular goodness and perfection. Each of the various creatures, willed in its own being, reflects in its own way a ray of God's infinite wisdom and goodness. Man must therefore respect the

particular goodness of every creature, to avoid any disordered use of things which would be in contempt of the Creator and would bring disastrous consequences for human beings and their environment. – Section 338

There is one particular feature of Polyface Farms which may be the most important. Polyface Farms is a four-generation working family farm. Many features of Polyface Farms have been seen and read about across the nation. Yet, the multi-generational family legacy on a working farm may be far more important than all the other wonderful aspects of Polyface.

Salatin emphasizes over and over the profound and multiple disconnects in our modern world. He correctly notes how we are out of sync with nature and natural growing systems. The factory food we consume even puts us out of sync with our very selves, as our health deteriorates from consuming a diet of unnatural products.

Cities tend to mold families into the grand disconnect. Modern family patterns frequently involve separate and independent work, commuting, learning, eating, and play. When they go to church, families are often segmented in various age groups.

How is the family in the modern world going to reconnect when so many facets of life seem disconnected? Where will the fundamental rebuilding of a multi-generational family culture take place? The English word "culture" is derived from a Latin word that literally means "cultivation." My suggestion is that an intelligently designed family farm may be one of the finest places to rebuild a family culture—from the ground up.

21st century sea-energy agriculture

The three farmers I've described who practice Intelligent Design Farming have obviously freed themselves from preconceived agricultural notions. If you are also going to break the mold, why not go all the way by practicing twenty-first century sea-energy agriculture?

Dr. Maynard Murray, a physician and research scientist during the later half of the twentieth century, relentlessly pursued ways to prevent degenerative diseases, especially cancer. His research led him to travel with fishermen in various parts of the world. What he didn't find at sea astonished him: cancer in the numerous types of saltwater fish he dissected. Dr. Murray knew that all fresh water trout develop terminal cancer of the liver around the age of five. In contrast, saltwater trout never get cancer. He also discovered that saltwater fish don't develop hardening of the arteries and a host of other common degenerative maladies.

After his discoveries at sea, Dr. Murray took to the lab. He tested laboratory mice bred to get breast cancer. The control group was fed normal grains, while the test group was fed grains grown with nutrients from ocean solids. Ninety percent of the control group developed cancer as predicted, while only fifty-five percent of the experimental group using sea minerals for fertilizers did. Dr. Murray then bred a second generation from the experimental group and fed them sea-minerals-enriched food. For that second generation, the cancer rate dropped to 2 percent.

What about humans? Dr. Murray found that population areas with low cancer rates were also locations with soils rich in trace minerals.[18] These minerals, often deemed optional and unimportant, are all found in the sea in a perfect balance with each other. Sea-water is chemically similar to the composition of human blood.

What's in the ocean that's not found in today's soils and fresh water? If you go to your garden supply store, you'll notice on the front of fertilizer bags three numbers representing the three major ingredients in the bag, namely nitrogen, phosphorus, and potassium (N-P-K). If you're looking at a quality fertilizer it might list a dozen or so minor elements. These essential elements are minor only in proportion to N-P-K. They could play a major role in your family's health, yet these trace minerals are often absent in today's soils. The ocean contains about ninety minerals. That is probably the ideal balance intelligently designed by our Creator.

Perhaps the easiest way to get nourishment from the sea to livestock is by offering them an organic sea-mineral product like Thorvin, a nutrient-rich kelp product. The Thorvin company makes the claim that it is the only kelp product with a guaranteed amount of selenium. Why is that important?

How a Family Can Begin Farming

I can't speak for all areas of the country, but a Clemson University veterinarian and lecturer said that southern soils are nearly devoid of selenium. This vet recounted how he was called to a farm to assist a newly-born calf whose owners thought was born diseased because it didn't have the strength to stand up. The farmers were amazed that a simple shot of selenium enabled the calf to get on its feet within thirty minutes.

Selenium is a micro-nutrient that animals and humans don't need much of (it's toxic in large quantities), but it's a requirement for optimium health.

In addition to providing kelp-minerals to animals, pastures nourished with sea-fertilizers result in healthy and vigorous livestock. Many families have already discovered the benefits of eating grass-fed meat; animals raised on sea-mineral fertilized pastures will muliply the increased health benefits to savvy consumers.

In case you don't want to wait for the sea-fertilizer grass-fed movement to develop, you can start today in your garden and in your kitchen. Non-hybrid tomatoes and sweet potatoes are good candidates for their ability to draw up trace nutrients from garden soil enriched with sea-fertilizer.

Wheat-grass juicing in a low-heat-producing juicer (don't use a high-speed juicer) provides almost all the benefits of ocean fertility. You can grow wheat-grass in a two-square-foot space near a window. Using a product like SEA90 sold by SeaAgri to enrich your wheat-grass could be your first step towards practicing twenty-first century agriculture and enhancing your family's health.[19] There are two good books on sea-fertilizers: *Fertility from the Ocean Deep* by Charles Walters and *Sea Energy Agriculture* by Maynard Murray. I recommend reading both of them as you develop your farming plans.[20]

Location, location, location

Before launching a farm venture it would be wise to give serious consideration to the long-term weather patterns in the location you select. I have been told that most of the principles of rotational mob-grazing are applicable anywhere

How a Family Can Begin Farming

in the United States. While that may be true, it is certainly going to be much easier to begin farming in a location with adequate rainfall and where the winters are temperate enough to avoid large quantities of costly supplemental feeding. It's worth investigating areas where the weather permits mostly year-round grazing.

Oregon State University's website has color-coded U.S. maps showing the thirty-year normal annual precipitation rates.[21] Pay attention to this map, especially if you plan to locate west of the Mississippi. Without water there is no life: plant or animal.

In addition to studying the amounts of rainfall, investigate the long-term drought cycles in the United States going back to 1900 at the Historic Palmer Drought Indicies at NOAA's National Climatic Center.[22] Droughts happen, and it is wise to know the long-term patterns you can expect in the area you are considering.

Remember, it's impossible to grow things without adequate water. Pick a farm location where God seems generous with his bounty of rain. Rain is his blessing for flourishing flocks and herds.

> "He covers the heavens with clouds, he prepares rain for the earth, he makes grass grow upon the hills. He gives to the beasts their food" (Psalm 147:8-9).

> "And he will give rain for the seed with which you sow the ground, and grain, the produce of the ground, which will be rich and plenteous. In that day your cattle will graze in large pastures" (Isaiah 30:23).

Getting started in any venture is challenging. Therefore, it would be a good idea to launch your flocks and herds in a year without an extreme winter and with adequate rainfall. A good source for the upcoming year's weather is *The Old Farmer's Almanac* (skip the astrology section). Its authors are seasoned enough to recognize that near-term and long-term oscillations in climate (i.e., climate change) are primarily dependent upon solar cycles, sunspot activity, and ocean-atmospheric patterns.

If you plan to direct-market your farm products, choose a farm location near an area with a sufficient population interested in buying and supporting locally grown food. Be aware that there is a wide price variable for locally grown food depending upon the location.

If you choose to follow Greg Judy's leasing strategy, you'll want to buy or rent a home in an area with multiple potential properties to lease. Also, be aware that in some locales wealthy retirees cluster and thus significantly drive up rural land prices. Most young families can't compete with wealthy retirees for country acreage.

Finally, just as your farm needs good weather to flourish, so your family requires a good parish. It's a good idea to choose an area with at least a couple of good churches within reasonable driving distance.

Grandfarming

Before becoming a grandfather, I declined numerous requests from grandparents for practical advice. I didn't feel up to the task of offering family advice when my only experience was what I read about in books. Now that I am a grandfather of eight, I do have some advice. If you are inclined and are in reasonably good health, then become a grandfarmer.

The Social Security Administration says that the life expectancy of a man reaching age sixty-five in the United States today is, on average, age eighty-four. In 1900 the average life expectancy was only forty-nine.

Grandparents today have over three decades of life that our ancestors a century ago didn't have. What better place is there than a farm to contribute to the physical development and spiritual formation of grandchildren? Can you think of a better or more rewarding way to spend the remaining decades of your life? Besides, working on a farm will undoubtedly contribute to your health and well-being.

Even if your grandchildren live at a distance, extended visits during the busy summer months for farming will provide a lifetime of memories and influences. My father lived in a small Iowa town, but it was working on a nearby farm during the summers that sparked his love for raising cattle.

What will your grandchildren be doing if they aren't outside working with you? Most likely, they will be playing video games all summer while scanning their smartphones during game breaks.

Richard Louv, in his book *Last Child in the Woods: Saving Our Children from Nature-Deficit Disorder*, highlights the sad statistic that between 1997 and 2003 there was a 50 percent decline in the proportion of time children aged nine to twelve spent in outdoor activities.[23] Grandfarming may be an effective way to reverse this alarming decline.

If grace truly builds upon nature, we need to ask ourselves, "What is happening to our children and grandchildren as members of the first generation being raised apart from meaningful contact with the natural world?"

The patron saint of farmers

Farming families should know that the patron saint of farmers is St. Isidore (1070 – 1130) of Madrid, Spain. St. Isidore, himself a farmer, was canonized in 1622 along with four other famous Spanish saints: St. Ignatius of Loyola, St. Teresa of Avila, St. Francis Xavier, and St. Phillip Neri. In Spain this group is known as "the five saints." St. Isidore's feast day is May 15th.

Surprising changes

If you become a grass farmer you might be surprised by a couple of unanticipated changes in your personal life.

First, you may find that a love for God's gift of the soil may grow on you. The Old Testament Israelite King Uzziah "hewed out many cisterns, for he had large herds . . . and he had farmers and vinedressers in the hills and in the fertile lands, *for he loved the soil*" (2 Chronicles 26:10).

Secondly, if you become a farmer, don't worry if you begin hearing things that you've never heard before. In fact, those with ears to hear may notice, especially around sunrise or sunset, the majestic chorus that our disconnected modern world's mad rush to nowhere is missing.

> "Let the field exult, and everything in it! Then shall all the trees of the wood sing for joy before the LORD" (Psalm 96:12-13).

A farmer's prayer of thanksgiving

I am happy to cooperate with You in Your
work of continuous creation, by growing the
food that men need to sustain life.
By Your almighty power You make grow
the seeds I plant. You fill the earth with
minerals,
You send the rain and the sun, the
wind and the snow—and the dry,
hard seeds I plant are raised to soft, green life.
I thank You again for choosing me to be
a farmer. I beg of You never to let me forget
its great advantages of closeness to You,
absolute trust and confidence in You, and
the fullness and richness of my life,
close to the earth that You have made
and have so marvelously blessed.
Lord, I am grateful that I am a farmer.
Amen.[24]

Farming, Faith, & Family Life

Psalm 23

The Lord is my shepherd, I shall not want;
>he makes me lie down in green pastures.

He leads me beside still waters;
>he restores my soul.

He leads me in paths of righteousness
>for his name's sake.

Even though I walk through the valley
>of the shadow of death, I fear no evil;
>for thou art with me;
>thy rod and thy staff, they comfort me.

Thou preparest a table before me
>in the presence of my enemies;
>thou anointest my head with oil,
>my cup overflows.

Surely goodness and mercy shall follow me
>all the days of my life;
>and I shall dwell in the house of the Lord
>for ever.

ENDNOTES

1   Visit the document libraries of www.ewtn.com. Enter a search for "rural life" to see the twelve documents available. See also, Fr. Denis Fahey, *The Church and Farming* (Palmdale, CA: Christian Book Club, 2002).

2   Pope Pius XII, speech delivered in Rome on November 15, 1946, to the delegates at the Convention of the National Confederation of Farm Owner-Operators (Des Moines, IA: National Catholic Rural Life Conference). Available online at: www.ewtn.com/library/PAPALDOC/POPRURAL.HTM.

3   *The Washington Times*, May 16, 2005, citing U.S. Department of Agriculture statistics.

4   Farm co-ops have imploded from unexpected divorces, pornography addictions, financial reversals, and other causes. The more families involved in ownership and decision-making, the greater the number of potential pitfalls.

5   Pope Pius XII, speech delivered in Rome on November 15, 1946, to the delegates at the Convention of the National Confederation of Farm Owner-Operators (Des Moines, IA: National Catholic Rural Life Conference).

6   Petroleum prices may also be a future factor in deciding the distance of your farm from a nearby community. Also remember that, as children get older, they may want to participate in more city activities such as sports teams, youth groups, and music lessons/ensembles. To counterbalance

closeness, consider that many suburban and metropolitan areas are rapidly expanding into the countryside. Choose a location that is not in the path of near-term growth, so that your farm isn't situated next to a Walmart within a decade.

7   Allan C. Carlson, *The New Agrarian Mind: The Movement Toward Decentralist Thought in Twentieth-Century America* (New Brunswick, NJ: Transaction Publishers, 2000). Don't overlook Carlson's conclusion on pages 212-214, where he describes homeschooling's revolutionary ability to refunctionalize the family. Carlson also has articles online about homeschooling and family life at www.profam.org. See also his *From Cottage to Work Station: The Family's Search for Social Harmony in the Industrial Age* (San Francisco, CA: Ignatius Press, 1993).

8   Carlson, *The New Agrarian Mind*, p. 213.

9   Don't get hung up with trying to find the best type of "pure farming." The type-of-farming question is important, but secondary. A careful analysis of the dynamics of what makes for a successful homeschool family life, including the counter-cultural religious motivations, is of primary importance.

10 Carlson, *The New Agrarian Mind*, p. 213.

11 John Senior, *The Restoration of Christian Culture* (San Francisco, CA: Ignatius Press, 1983), pp. 220—222.

12 Carlson, *The New Agrarian Mind,* p. 171.

13 C.S. Lewis, *The Abolition of Man* (New York, NY: Macmillan Publishing, New York, 1947), p. 82.

Endnotes

14 Greg Judy's farm: www.greenpasturesfarm.net/index.php

15 The 12 Aprils dairy grazing program: www.happycowcreamery.com/12-aprils-program/

16 Happy Cow Creamery: www.happycowcreamery.com/

17 Polyface Farms: www.polyfacefarms.com/

18 Charles Walters, *Fertility from the Ocean Deep*, (Austin, TX: Acres U.S.A., 2012), page 69.

19 Sea90 fertilizer. www.seaagri.com/

20 Walters, *Fertility from the Ocean Deep* and Maynard Murray, *Sea Energy Agriculture* (Austin, TX: Acres U.S.A., 2003).

21 Oregon State's 30-year precipitation rates. www.prism.oregonstate.edu/normals/

22 NOAA's Historic Palmer Drought Indicies. www.ncdc.noaa.gov/temp-and-precip/drought/historical-palmers/.

23 Richard Louv, *Last Child in the Woods:Saving Our Children from Nature-Deficit Disorder* (Chapel Hill, NC: Algonquin Books, 2008), p. 34.

24 A prayer from the *The Rural Life Prayerbook* published by The National Catholic Rural Life Conference in 1956. Republished by Tan Publishers, 2014. Used by permission.

Farming, Faith, & Family Life

Recommended Reading

Acres USA. To learn about this informative monthly magazine visit www.acresusa.com. Individual copies of *Acres* are available at Tractor Supply. Many of the authors featured in *Acres* have produced YouTube videos for free viewing.

Carlson, Allan C. *The Natural Family Where It Belongs: New Agrarian Essays*. New Brunswick, NJ: Transaction Publishers, 2014. This book is essential reading when considering the impact of farming upon your family life. It presents a hopeful view of how the twenty-first-century family can thrive in the new agrarianism.

Carlson, Allan C. *The New Agrarian Mind: The Movement Toward Decentralist Thought in Twentieth-Century America*. New Brunswick, NJ: Transaction Publishers, 2000. The final pages of this book offer invaluable lessons on the principal causes of the failure of the twentieth-century New Agrarian project.

Davis, Walt. *How to Not Go Broke Ranching: Things I Learned the Hard Way in Fifty Years of Ranching*. Charleston, SC: CreateSpace Publishing, 2011. A no-nonsense guide to raising healthy, economical, efficient, and stress-free livestock on flourishing pasture.

Grodi, Marcus. *Life from Our Land: The Search for a Simpler Life in a Complex World*. San Francisco, CA: Ignatius Press,

2015. At the heart of Christian discipleship is transformation into the image of Christ. To discover such a profound life change, seekers often head to conferences, renewal centers, or foreign pilgrimages. Marcus Grodi experienced, as John Senior predicted, a remarkable spiritual transformation by simply integrating his faith life with working on a farm. Those seeking to unearth a vision of life change and purpose will find treasures in these pages.

Judy, Greg. *No Risk Ranching: Custom Grazing on Leased Land*. Ridgeland, MI: Green Park Press, 2002. Judy's two books are the best resources for any family who wishes to make a profit and avoid going broke while farming. It's recommended that you read Judy *before* buying land and expensive farm equipment.

Judy, Greg. *Comeback Farms: Rejuvenating Soils, Pastures and Profits with Livestock Grazing Management*. Ridgeland, MI: Green Park Press, 2008. Greg Judy's books can be purchased from the *Acres USA* store and from www.greenpasturesfarm.net.

Logsdon, Gene. *The Contrary Farmer*. White River Junction, VT: Chelsea Green Publishing Company, 1994.

Manyard Murray, *Sea Energy Agriculture: Nature's Ideal Trace Element Blend for Farm, Livestock, Humans*. Austin, TX: Acres U.S.A., 2003.

Ramsey, Dave, *The Total Money Makeover: A Proven Plan for Financial Fitness*. Nashville, TN, Thomas Nelson, 2007. The audio book CD version is more motivational than the

Recommended Reading

printed edition. Thoroughly digest Dave Ramsey if you are tempted to go into debt for your farming venture.

Salatin, Joel. *Folks, This Ain't Normal: A Farmer's Advice for Happier Hens, Healthier People, and a Better World.* New York, NY: Hatchette Book Group, Inc., 2011.

Salatin, Joel. *You Can Farm: The Entrepreneur's Guide to Start & Succeed in a Farming Enterprise.* Swoope, VA: Polyface, Inc., 1998.

The Stockman Grass Farmer. 2012. A free sample issue is available upon request at www.stockmangrassfarmer.com.

Walters, Charles. *Fertility from the Ocean Deep.* Austin, TX: Acres U.S.A., 2012.

About the Author

Steve Wood spent his childhood on Woodlane Farm. The farm's Angus herd, along with President Eisenhower's, were the top two herds in Pennsylvania and surrounding states. At twelve years-old, Steve won the Lehigh Valley 4-H heifer grand championship in both confirmation and showmanship. In his twenties, he was a Certified Florida Horticulturist before becoming an Evangelical pastor.

In 1990, he and his family entered the Catholic Church. Since then he has been the president of the Family Life Center International, which seeks to promote faith, fatherhood, and family life in over a hundred countries worldwide. He is the longtime host of *Faith & Family Radio,* heard on stations around the country and worldwide through podcasting. Steve is the author of two books on Christian fatherhood and two books on courtship and marriage preparation.

In 2015, Steve began raising a flock of grass-fed St. Croix sheep on his Good Shepherd Heritage Farm in Greenville, SC.